CONEY ISLAND
KALEIDOSCOPE

Front cover: *Wonder Wheel at Night*

CONEY ISLAND KALEIDOSCOPE

PHOTOGRAPHY BY
LYNN HYMAN BUTLER

TEXT BY
JOHN B. MANBECK

FOREWORD BY
CHARLES-HENRI FAVROD

Beautiful America Publishing Company

Published by
Beautiful America Publishing Company©
P.O. Box 646
Wilsonville, Oregon 97070

Design: Michael Brugman
Illustration: Horace Bullard
French translation: Shary Grossman
Linotronic output: LeFont Typography

CONEY ISLAND KALEIDOSCOPE

Library of Congress Cataloging-in-publication Data
Butler, Lynn Hyman, 1953-
Coney Island Kaleidoscope / photography by Lynn H. Butler;
text by John B. Manbeck; foreword by Charles Henri Favrod.
ISBN 0-89802-569-9;   ISBN 0-89802-566-4 (pbk.)
1. Coney Island (New York, N.Y.)—History.
2. Coney Island (New York, N.Y.)—History—Pictorial works.
I. Manbeck, John B., 1931-. II. Title.
GV1853.3.N72C663 1991   791'.06'874723—dC20
90-27277 CIP

Copyright 1991 by Beautiful America Publishing Co.©
Photography copyright by Lynn H. Butler
Text copyright by John B. Manbeck
Illustration copyright by Horace Bullard
Archive photograph courtesy of
Kingsborough Historical Society
All Rights Reserved
No portion of this book is to be reproduced
without written permission from the publisher.

Printed in Hong Kong

To my mother, Barbara Hyman
and my father, Dr. George Hyman

ACKNOWLEDGMENTS

I would like to thank John Manbeck for his painstaking research and wonderful enthusiasm in writing about an important part of American history.

I would like to thank David Grey for his help in printing my photographs for the book as well as for exhibitions, and Horace Bullard for his dreams of rebuilding Steeplechase Park and his interest in my work in rekindling interest in the plight of Coney Island.

I would also like to express my appreciation to Ruby Jacobs from Coney Island and Mildred Otten (a Fine Arts collector) for their support and encouragement.

Lynn Hyman Butler

CONTENTS

Foreword (english) viii

Préface (french) x

Introduction 1

Coney Island Mood 3

Amusements 6

The Boardwalk 72

Food and Drink 81

The Beach 90

Surrounding Communities 98

Coney Island Experience 101

Afterward: The Future 106

FOREWORD

Coney Island was called Conynge Hook by the Dutch when they arrived one morning in September 1609 on board the *Half-Moon*, commanded by the English captain, Hudson, who gave his name to the river after thinking it was an arm of the sea and a passage through which one could eventually reach the Pacific and China. In 1626, the French-born Peter Minuit bought from the Algonquin or Mohawk Indians the island called Manhattan for 24 dollars, payable in glass beads. A stockade fence would soon cross it to protect cattle from bears and wolves, the area we know today as Wall Street.

Coney Island was for a long time the elegant beach resort of New York. Old prints and photographs of the 19th Century show fine gentlemen who, even then, played with dice with fellows in caps. And the women, with parasols and cashmere shawls, watched paddleboats and sailboats come and go. But soon the masses arrived, chasing the rich to Long Island. And the subway poured forth the crowds of Brooklyn, then all of New York, towards the increasing attractions; the roller coaster and the Ferris wheel. With the help of electricity it could always be daytime in Coney Island, with lights and projectors creating for the whirling throng a street fair around the various booths, with games of chance, Barbary organs, and, soon, jukeboxes. Consumers of hamburgers and hot dogs, oysters and clams and many spectacles, starting with midgets and bearded ladies, sword swallowers and fire eaters, Negroes and Chinamen, and bathers who dared to show more and more of their nude bodies. This Luna Park so bleak in winter, but so animated in summer being by the seashore, was a unique place in the world. How could it be otherwise when it was the beach for the most extraordinary city, with a mixture of the most diverse populations that ever came together?

One is, therefore, not surprised that it figures often in literature and that the Beat generation felt more at home there than anywhere else. In 1958, Lawrence Ferlinghetti published *The Coney Island of the Mind.* Jack Kerouac introduced it to Robert Frank who returned there with Diane Arbus. But photographers had made it their subject since the 19th Century, as I have already said, and now it is time to celebrate over again photography, which captures a moment in time so useful for history and nostalgia. But which permits us also to grasp things through the sensibility of each photographer, proof that the same subject can inspire totally different images.

That is why the work of Lynn Butler affected me so much. Her approach is completely unique. Firstly, in the use of color, which treats in an Impressionistic manner that which has often been treated in a documentary fashion. She introduces an element of mystery, which is inherent in Coney Island, tied to the accidents of experience one finds there, the surprises which are always part of such a mix of different people. She catches the incident which is always possible, in which tragedy can exist side by side with festivity. And she celebrates the incomparable, ever-changing and unexpected light, which is sometimes like the famous Coney Island aquarium in which one finds a teeming mixture of fish.

What I like most of all is that no one has ever before shown this place in this manner. Lynn Butler modified the approach to it completely. It is another place which she shows, and yet one recognizes all that one sees there. That is the importance of her work, all the more so, since one could be tempted to think one could only repeat oneself by photographing Coney Island after so many others have done it. She demonstrates, therefore, that photography has not stopped provoking surprises when the photographer does not limit himself to following in the footsteps of his predecessors. There is no such thing as a banal subject for he who is gifted with the ability to see, and the imagination to express himself in imagery, to the extent of revealing unreality in the real world.

I am sure that all who discover the work of Lynn Butler will join with me in celebrating the poetic novelty of her vision and will no longer be able to see Coney Island in any other way. This is the task which she has set herself and which she has carried out so marvelously well.

Charles-Henri Favrod
Director of the Museé de l'Elysée
The Swiss Museum of Photography
Lausanne, Switzerland

PREFACE

Coney Island fut le Conynge Hook des Hollandais quand ils y arrivèrent un matin de septembre 1609, à bord du *Demi-Lune*, commandé par le capitaine anglais Hudson qui donna son nom à la rivière après avoir cru qu'il s'agissait d'un bras de mer et du passage permettant d'atteindre enfin le Pacifique et la Chine. En 1626, Peter Minuet, d'origine française, achète aux Indiens Algonquins ou Mohawks leur île de Manhattan pour 24 dollars payables en perles de verre. Un mur de pieux va bientôt la traverser pour protéger le bétail des ours et des loups, qui est comme on sait aujourd'hui Wall Street.

Coney Island fut longtemps la plage élégante de New York. D'anciennes gravures et des photographies du XIXe siècle montrent des messieurs en haut de forme qui, déjà, jouent aux dés avec des gars en casquette. Et des dames, avec ombrelle et châle en cachemire, regardent aller et venir des bateaux à roues ou à voiles. Mais bientôt arrive le peuple qui va chasser les riches vers Long Island. Et le métro déverse la foule de Brooklyn, puis de tout New York vers les attractions qui se multiplient, dont les montagnes russes et la grande roue. L'électricité aidant, il fera toujours jour à Coney Island, lampions et projecteurs pour une cohue foraine autour des baraques, des machines à sous, des orgues de Barbarie et bientôt des juke-boxes. Mangeurs de hamburgers et de saucisses, d'huîtres et de clams, et tant de phénomènes, à commencer par les nains et les femmes à barbe, les avaleurs de sabre et les cracheurs de feu, les Noirs et les Chinois, les dactylos et les mauvais garçons, et les baigneurs qui s'enhardissent de plus en plus à montrer leur corps nus. Ce Luna-Park, si triste en hiver, mais dont l'animation d'été, au bord de l'océan, fait un lieu unique au monde. Comment en serait-il autrement puisqu'il s'agit de la plage de la ville la plus extraordinaire et du plus grand rassemblement de populations diverses jamais opéré?

On ne peut donc s'étonner que la littérature en ait fait des morceaux de bravoure et que la beat generation s'y soit sentie plus à l'aise qu'ailleurs. En 1958, Lawrence Ferlinghetti publie *The Coney Island of the Mind*. Jack Kerouac fait découvrir les lieux à Robert Frank, qui y retournera avec Diane Arbus. Mais bien des photographes en ont fait leur sujet dès le XIXe siècle, comme je l'ai dit déjà, et c'est l'occasion de célébrer une fois de plus la photographie qui dresse un état momentané si utile à l'histoire et à la nostalgie. Mais qui permet aussi d'appréhender les choses à travers la sensibilité de chaque photographe, preuve que des sujets identiques peuvent donner des images différentes et infiniment complémentaires.

C'est pourquoi le travail de Lynn Hyman Butler m'a touché si fort. En effet, son approche est tout à fait particulière. D'abord par le traitement de la couleur qui restitue de manière impressionniste ce qu'on a souvent traité sur le mode documentaire. Elle introduit une part de mystère qui est d'ailleurs inhérente à Coney Island, liée au hasard des rencontres qu'on y fait, des surprises qui sont toujours ménagées par l'afflux des gens divers. Elle fait percevoir l'incident toujours possible, puisque le drame peut surgir à côté de la fête. Et puis elle y célèbre la lumière qui est incomparable, changeante, inattendue et parfois comme celle du fameux aquarium de Coney où frémissent les murènes, les petites baleines blanches et les poissons panthères.

Ce que j'aime surtout, c'est qu'on n'a jamais encore montré cet endroit de cette manière. Lynn Hyman Butler en modifie complètement l'approche. C'est comme un autre lieu qu'elle montre et pourtant on y reconnaît tout ce qu'on y a pu voir. C'est dire la nécessité de son travail, d'autant plus qu'on serait tenté de penser qu'on ne peut que se répéter en photographiant après tant d'autres à Coney Island. Elle démontre donc que la photographie n'a pas fini de provoquer des surprises quand le photographe veut bien ne pas se borner à mettre ses pas dans ceux d'autres qui l'ont précédé. Il n'y a pas de sujet banal pour qui est doté de la puissance du regard et dont l'imagination s'exprime en images au point de révéler l'irréalité du réel.

Je suis convaincu que tous ceux qui vont découvrir le travail de Lynn Hyman Butler seront d'accord avec moi pour en célébrer la nouveauté poétique et ne pourront désormais plus voir Coney Island autrement. C'était le pari qu'elle s'était donné et qu'elle a merveilleusement bien tenu.

Charles-Henri Favrod
Conservateur de Musée de l'Elysée,
un musée pour la photographie,
Lausanne, Switzerland

Surf Avenue West, Coney Island, 1912

INTRODUCTION

Coney Island is real.

It isn't phantasmagoria.

One of the more popular attractions of early Coney Island was the "camera obscura," a box-like room from which customers could see images of external objects projected in color onto a white disc through an aperture and a curved lens. The shapes looked real enough to the visitors of this pre-television age—but they weren't.

Reality is the permanence of Coney Island, but a layer of illusion always accompanied that reality.

For over 347 years, the land projection off the southern edge of Kings County, a.k.a. Brooklyn, has affected lives of both inhabitants and visitors. Originally a fishing cove, burial ground and source of Indian wampum, it became a grazing field for the cattle of the Gravesend residents when the Brooklyn townships were established. Although in an ideal location for the resort it became, Gravesend was ten miles from Manhattan and the furthest community to the south. Only with the development of adequate public transportation could the community flourish. Travel finally blossomed in the 1870s with steam trains and steam boats regularly routed to Coney Island.

Part of the mystical attraction of Coney Island may be its association with the triad, Number Three. Originally, the island was divided into three land masses, each of them islands; three eras of Coney's giddy life can be divided among the primitive, until 1870; the golden age, 1880-1915; and The Nickel Empire, 1915-1965. The coda, the period since the 1960s, has yet to be identified.

Three social classes lined themselves along the sands from west to east: the working class coupled with the criminal element settled at West End; the middle class were attracted to West Brighton, the heart of the amusement section; and the rich made themselves comfortable in the east at the hotels of Manhattan Beach.

Three race tracks provided entertainment for the rich and gamblers, while three amusement parks—Steeplechase, Luna Park and Dreamland—amused the average visitors who were transported on public vehicles: steamships, trains and trolley cars.

Today the amusement nucleus has dwindled to about ten scarred blocks. And that's not illusion, either. On page xii there is an archival photograph of old Coney Island; further on is the reality of today's Coney, as interpreted through Lynn Butler's Nikon camera.

It's not the camera obscura, but "Step right up!" anyway.

CONEY ISLAND MOOD

hange?

Coney Island has changed.

But then, the more things change, the more they remain the same.

Coney Island has always been an outpost, a place where people let inhibitions escape, a place to escape to. Coney Island hasn't changed—neither have the people who go there. Like the rides that spin into kaleidoscopic hues and multiple images, Coney Island has remained the hub to the swiftly passing human scene.

This two and one-half mile patch of sand on the southern shore of Brooklyn between Gravesend and Jamaica Bays is an icon of the motion seen in the photographic art work of Lynn Butler. It shrunk from its original five miles but has weathered storms of nature as well as storms of protest. Tides and erosion have torn the island apart and reconstructed it; humans have fought tribal and political wars over the territory; some of the most progressive, imaginative and flamboyant ideas have been created on its shores.

Coney Island is the pulse of movement.

But, while its rhythm has been steady, its growth has been uncontrolled. In the last century, hundreds of cubicle-like bath houses—smaller than closets—dotted the sands of Coney Island. During the periodic fires that swept the community, the shacks burned, to be replaced by ornate privately-owned bathing pavilions and hotels built down to the waterline; more recently, wooden walks that stretched to the sea separated the private bungalows. "Amusement" rides were created from madmen's nightmares.

Only when nature retaliated with a decade of winter fury was there an attempt to organize Coney Island logically. Entrepreneurs gathered the best rides into three gigantic walled parks: Steeplechase, Luna Park (built on the remains of Sea Lion Park, Coney Island's first), and

Dreamland.

Luna, the popular favorite, with the Shoot-the-Chutes kingpin attraction, was an ingenious creation of mystique, glamour and thrills. Steeplechase, the longest-lived park, twisted the customers' attitudes of fun with its Whirlpool, Vomit Pit and Insanitarium. Dreamland, a corporate creation, developed into a short-lived pristine duplicate of Luna. These parks were the core of the Golden Age of Coney Island, which lasted from 1895 until the mid- 1950s, with 1909 the pinnacle year.

In 1938, *Fortune*, a business magazine, tabulated the number of private enterprises located in Coney Island: 13 carousels, 70 ball games, 11 roller coasters, 5 tunnel rides, 3 fun houses, 2 waxworks, 6 penny arcades, 20 shooting galleries, 3 freak shows, 200 eating establishments—over 500 businesses. In a season, 25 million visitors spent from $7 to $35 million there.

Then came a zealous parks commissioner who strove to destroy the tawdry aspects of Coney Island, to bring the beach back to the people, and to transform the shoreline into a residential community.

In this, fortunately, Robert Moses failed.

Ironically, the seamy side either brightened into garishness or faded into shadowy substance. But the vibrancy of life survived. More people have been drawn to Coney Island over the years that to any other New York attraction; Coney Island has outlasted all other amusement areas in America and most in the world. From the shadows of the Cyclone, the Thunderbolt, the Parachute Jump, Stauch's Baths, Child's Restaurant still drifts the spirit of all that Coney Island represented; the crowds that still flock to the seaside at Coney Island show that the change has wrought more of the same.

Only the faces have really changed.

Bathers Under Parachute Jump

AMUSEMENTS

Faces of people emerging from rides are special, full of clues, whether the ride be a subway car or a roller coaster. At their destination, they reveal expectation, satisfaction, success.

The roller coaster is the essence of rail transportation, a monstrously comic version of the train: wheels placed on rails so that container-like vehicles could travel smoothly between two points. Used to transport people at the middle of the nineteenth century, trains had also been used in mines to assist with the removal of ore.

Rail transportation turned into elevateds and the "L" grew loops and whirls. Subways followed as rides through dripping grottoes. Then trolleys. A writer observed that a man who suffered in a trolley ride what he endured at Coney Island would be committed to a sanitarium for life and would sue the trolley company. The Cyclone, a product of 1928 in spite of its wooden frame, and the most famous ride in Coney Island, was embroiled in legalities more recently.

Threatened with demolition and closed for lack of insurance premiums, The Cyclone survived the challenges and continues to be a classic of a business in which the latest upside-down, double-twist, twenty-story free fall technology is taking the original 1880 invention by LaMarcus Adna Thompson to the threshold of space travel. Visitors from around the world travel to Coney Island to ride this veteran of the original amusement park. Where the roller coaster was created in 1884 under the name switchback railway and where once a Thompson Scenic Railway ran on almost every Coney Island corner, now only The Cyclone remains.

The shell of the Thunderbolt lies rusting several blocks away, awaiting demolition crews; the Tornado burned and is long gone.

The names of former roller coasters live in

the pages of history books but connote clear images: at Luna Park–The Dragon's Gorge, Cannon Coaster, Mile High Sky Chaser, The Toboggan; at Dreamland–Over the Great Divide, Coasting Through Switzerland, The Great Deep Rift Coal Mine of Pennsylvania, Leap Frog Railway (two cars ride toward each other on a single track); at Steeplechase–the Comet, Coaster Figure Eight; at Feltman's Restaurant–Flying Boat Roller Coaster and Ziz; and the independent roller coasters along Surf Avenue–Shaw Channel Chute; Jackman's Thriller; Drop the Dip; Roosevelt's Rough Riders; Rocky Road to Dublin, the ill-fated coaster to which lions fled in the 1911 fire at Dreamland; The Great Whirlwind Ride; the Whirlfly, an insect-like car that moved around vertically as it rolled; Touring the Alps; Pike's Peak Railway; Red Devil Rider; and the Giant Racer, a double roller coaster that antedated The Cyclone on West 10th Street.

And these were just the roller coaster rides!

Imagine the excitement, the anticipation of the new rides that premiered each spring. Some shot in and out of cavern-like tunnels. Some passed through exotic, painted locales. Some had brakemen standing behind the rear car to prevent too much speed. Now, only arms raised overhead on The Cyclone attempt to forestall gravity's inevitable pull. Some visitors—listening to the clattering cog chain and studying the wooden superstructure—are disheartened before they reach the ticket booth. Tough veterans smirk, though, and race for the front car.

Other rail rides are slower but—like today's Hell Hole—attempt to frighten passengers into each other's arms: "You Who Enter Here, Abandon Hope." For today's visitor, the Tunnel of Love or The Old Mill ride is too tame. Even Steeplechase's original mechanized horse race would be a drag. Astroland's flume boat ride may be faster than the Shoot-the-Chutes, but not higher; but then

Roller Coaster at Night

The Red Horse

Luna also had the Mountain Torrent, a boat- roller coaster in a chute, and Dreamland built Hell Gate, a whirlpool ride in which boats descended on troughs. Hell Gate is where the 1911 fire started while workmen repaired the trough. Now, the Aquarium stands on the site.

Where visitors to the Aquarium today park their cars, once stood the Iron Tower, a 300-foot iron observation tower, purchased from the 1876 American Centennial Fair in Philadelphia. With the exception of hot air balloons tethered at Manhattan Beach, this was the highest altitude early visitors could reach. Many were fearful of the newly invented Otis steam elevators and preferred to walk up the steps.

Now there is the sealed-cabin safety of AstroTower with its glassed-in prisoners, but a sense of nostalgia can be evoked by the Wonder Wheel. The Wonder Wheel, of course, is a complex Ferris Wheel, one of the largest in this country, but minuscule compared to the original created in Chicago.

Memories lurk deepest in the western fringe of the amusement area. There broods the landmarked Parachute Jump, bought by the Tilyou family in 1941 from the Lifesaver exhibit at the 1939-40 New York World's Fair in Flushing Meadow, Queens. Although the Coney Island ride was used to train the military before its arrival in New York, parachutes had been around amusement parks before airplanes were invented. An early Tilyou ride called Dew Drop was a variation of the parachute with customers jumping off a ledge. In the twentieth century version, visitors would climb a tower and jump off strapped to an umbrella-like float. Today, parachute rides are more complicated. The Coney Island one simulated a certain degree of terror.

Customers, feet dangling freely but tightly belted at the waist with a single strap, swayed between the guide wires as the spider-like umbrella rose; a magnificent view of the city skyline, away from the hubbub of The Bowery and then—a clatter as the mechanism struck the top, sudden free fall, and a yank, guaranteed to shake you from the metal seat as the parachute billowed, another jerk as the ground rushed up to you and then you swung above the platform waiting to be released.

Smiles of relief or determined grins, depending whether you were going to repeat the experience or move on to other amusements.

Steeplechase, with its mechanical rides and jokes bringing simultaneous excitement and laughter to customers, appealed to the working class. "10 hours of fun for 10 cents," was an initial advertisement; later, the price increased along with the time. Opening daily (except Monday) at 1 in the afternoon, it crowded 28 rides into 12 acres of fun until midnight. At the end of the Steeplechase Pier, the 3-masted schooner "Saranac" was permanently moored. The most popular show was the Blowhole Theater at the end of the steeplechase ride. Women were led to the exit by clowns only to be positioned over jets of air which blew their dresses over their heads to the guffaws of the men leering from benches. Men would have their hats blown off or might be goosed by an electric cattle prod.

How about the merry-go-round?

The horses are still ferocious, teeth bared, exaggerated, gold-leaf manes flying whether standing, prancing or jumping. You can almost see the flecks of foam flying from their mouths. Multi-colored with jeweled straps, trappings and painted saddle blankets. Here is one armored for battle—but with an incongruous portrait of Lincoln on the blanket. But the clatter of their hooves is lost in the music from the WurliTzer carousel band organ in the center. Mirrors catch the rise and

AstroTower

The View from Below

fall of the horses, reflecting the jeweled bits; squeals of delight as the ring feeder swings into place. Then the winner, and the basket to return the rings. The drum thumps slower as the lights and colors drift into focus.

Years ago, creation of carousels was an art: hand-carved and hand-painted steeds were born in the mind of carver Mike Illions and mechanism evolved in William Mangels' machine-works factory on West 5th Street. Charles Looff started the business in 1876; the trade was taught in Germany.

Horses were not the only animals in the menagerie: there were saddled lions, zebras made from the mold of mules, jumping pigs, running rams, giraffes, ostriches, deer with real antlers, storks, panthers pulling chariots with portraits of American heroes in the center; stained-glass windows on top diffused more colors. Any imaginable animal—and a few from mythology—might be found in Coney Island carousels. Looff created the hippocampus, a half-horse, half-fish. Originally, these beasts sold for $35 each; now auctions price them at $35,000.

The El Dorado, a 3-deck carousel that was built for Kaiser Wilhelm II of Germany, was almost burned in the Dreamland fire. Now it lives in Tokyo. The Chanticleer with its flock of chickens added a sort of barnyard majesty outside the Steeplechase Pavilion of Fun. The B&B Carousell, the last at Coney Island, was built by Mangels and carved by Charles Carmel. At Coney Island, there were more merry-go-rounds than roller coasters.

Carousels are one of the oldest amusement rides, dating back hundreds of years. In Europe, children pushed simple playground carousels around with their feet. Before steam power developed, large ones were pulled by mules or ponies attached to the center post.

Other circular rides grew from this, such as

the Human Roulette Wheel, The Whichaway, The Circle Swing, The Scrambler, The Bumps, Virginia Reel and the Bug. The Tickler and The Whip were built by Coney Island native, William Mangels while the McCullough family created Tilyou's Razzle Dazzle. Airplane rides followed: The Gyroplane and Flying Turns which dipped and swooped. The Velodrome had bicycles that pursued each other on a circular track; Dodgem bumper cars sent drivers careering as they jolted around a metal course. Today, the Eldorado Auto Skooters are psychological light years away commanding riders to "Bump Your Ass Off." Astroland now has the kiddies buzzing in mutant insects. Of course, the faster the ride goes, the dizzier the customers get.

Disorientation is the name of the game. There were slides and collapsing stairs and wobbly floors. And the huge vertical wheel built by George Washington Ferris in seven months for the Chicago Columbia Exposition of 1892. Capable of holding 60 passengers—half of the seated in plush-covered swivel chairs—in each of its cars for a total of 2,000 riders (including guards in each car), it so impressed George Tilyou, a visitor honeymooning in Chicago, that he immediately ordered a copy of the model for the front yard of his father's hotel in Coney Island.

So it was that the first Ferris Wheel came to Brooklyn.

By comparison, the Wonder Wheel which came there in 1920 only holds 150 seated passengers, but it has another uniquely disorienting feature: alternate cars slide into the infinity of space. Today's guards are canines.

How about something peaceful like the Eden Wax Musee?

Or the freak show?

Or a game of chance?

The hustlers sounded their chants: barkers

Steeplechase Park Mural

Mural of Hell Hole

with their ballyhoo. And the catchpenny stands try to enchant you with a worthless bauble to remind you how much money you wasted. They are part of the Coney Island scene today as they were over a hundred years ago.

Nothing changes.

For hundreds of years, Coney Island had been divided: divided from the mainland, then subdivided into three major islands which eventually regrouped joining to form one land mass. Originally, the five-mile island boasted grape vines, cedar groves, wildlife and hills. It was governed by the neighboring Town of Gravesend, but not very closely, for shortly after dirt roads connected it to the mainland, the "sand waste" of dunes and sedge grass became the refuge for clammers, fishermen, poor families, salvagers of wrecks on the Rockaway Shoals, and criminals.

Slowly, with the arrival of steamboats, a summer community of sorts began to grow along the two miles of ocean front with a few hotels, pavilions—tent-like structures with roofs and curtained sides—where food was sold, a profusion of solitary bath houses, and music played by "negro minstrels or the organ- grinder," as a local paper noted. No "lady" would stay there overnight.

Then, with a miraculous burst of growth, the steam train arrived and, by the 1880s, there suddenly were eight steam railways, nine lines of steamboats, three main roadways, huge bath houses built on piers, pavilions capable of feeding 20,000, over 30 hotels and professional entertainers—all within eleven miles of Manhattan.

In ways, Coney Island was still divided: to the west was the undesirable, rowdy section alternately called West End, Coney Island or Norton's. The middle, more populous amusement section was West Brighton Beach; we identify the area today in the vicinity of Stillwell and Surf Avenues.

The Brighton reference made it more respectable. East of West Brighton was a more middle class locale named Brighton Beach, home of a race track and a grand hotel. Finally, at the eastern tip was the posh Manhattan Beach with formal band concerts, fireworks extravaganzas and two grander hotels.

From these beginnings, the amusement center that is famous world-wide grew—and grew, and grew so that 50 years later, millions still were drawn to its shores. Known for the excitement and a touch of evil it generated, it never achieved respectability among proper society although it strove for a place as a permanent world's fair midway.

Then, almost as suddenly as it blossomed, it withered, reduced to a ten-block amusement center flanked on the south by the still-expansive city beach. Today, many see it as threatened and threatening, but a surprising number of visitors still gravitate there every summer, drawn by the same forces that have always attracted New Yorkers during the hot season—cool, bathing water.

Guess your weight, miss? Not an ounce over 98 pounds, I bet...Lemme guess your birthday. You must be an Aquarius...Yo, check it out. Hit the bell. Lessee how strong you really are, mon...Your fortune, madam. I see a change in your life. The stars know all. Let the tarot cards read your future...Hit the bullseye, mac, win a bunny for your hunny...Round and round she goes. Take a chance on the wheel of fortune. Pick the lucky number and win any prize on the top shelf...

Coney has always had a soft spot for the catchpenny and the ballyhoo. The first visitors to the sandy beaches were harangued on the steamboats by pitchmen who sold smoked glasses for protection against the sun and hat cords so bon-

Michael the Tattoo Man

Tattoo Contest

Waiting in Line

Ride Operator

The Test of Strength

Inferno

The Snake Charmer

Entrance to Hell Hole

Teenagers Meeting

28 AMUSEMENTS

The Midget

Parading into Ruby's Bar

Lovers at Ruby's

The Sword Swallower

Breakdancing

Carrousel and Bumblebee

Dancing Under the Parachute Jump

Pink Horses

nets and skimmers would not fly away on the ocean breezes. On shore, salesmen with shovels and pails and food for picnic lunches or spiels for pony rides and acrobatic shows descended on the sidewheelers as they docked at Norton's or the Iron Pier. So many hucksters flooded the sands that bathers had to fight their way to the ocean.

Rifle ranges with moving animals and glass bubbles as well as target practice ranges were popular attractions, although sights were often misaligned to defeat true marksmen. Today the bullets shoot pellets and the guns are automatic. "Crazy Jack" Schaeffer, a Coney Island character, made a profession out of painting targets for the shooting galleries. "Aunt Sallies" were the predecessors of today's baseball pitch where the customer attempts to hit a target or knock over a pyramid of wooden bottles with a baseball. ("You must knock all bottles off the shelf.") Before World War II, many of the concessionaires were Japanese-Americans. Today's targets are the open mouths of plastic clown faces attached to balloons that fill with water. Skill and strength were the keywords for Coney Island sideshows.

The Bowery, from a Dutch word meaning "garden," was the most popular promenade for those visiting arcades, shooting galleries, cafes with variety shows, freak shows and dance halls. It became a site for young men and women to stroll, flirt and demonstrate their physical prowess. At first, men would test their lung power by blowing into a rubber tube; decades later they had to produce more substantial physical evidence at the high striker as athletics and gymnastics began to dominate the Victorian mind.

A typical scene:

The young man in the derby shucked off his jacket, folded it carefully and handed it to the woman in the straw hat and long shirtwaist dress. He loosened his collar pin, his vest buttons and

Hell Hole at Night

38 AMUSEMENTS

Coaster Over Stauch's Baths

pushed his sleeve garters up his arms. Then, taking the bulky rubber-headed sledgehammer from the attendant, he lifted it over his head to judge the weight, while the young lady stepped back with her fingers to her cupid-bowed lips. "One," cried the young man in the cap, wearing a change apron around his waist. The lever rose three-quarters up the scale. Passersby paused to watch, some women fanning themselves with Japanese fans. "Two," the crowd echoed the attendant. "One more try," he sneered. "Let's see if he's really a man or a pansy." More parasoled women stopped to watch. Perspiration beaded on the young man's brow. His mustache frowned. The woman gasped and looked away as he swung the hammer up and down before lifting it high over his head. The meter zoomed up the scale. "Clang!" went the bell, as the clapper slammed into it. The crowd cheered, the woman blushed and the young man, cocky and smiling, accepted a porcelain kewpie doll. "Oh," pouted the woman, "but I so wanted that canary there," as she pointed at the wooden cage. But then she looked down at the doll, smiled, and linked her arm in his as other men stepped forward.

In the 1940s, penny arcades featured "test-your-strength" handgrips, love potency scales and peep show cameras next to the veiled automaton grandmother willing to tell your fortune. Managers gave away boxes of candy "worth at least a dollar."

Today, jocks grit their teeth at a mechanical strong man in the same Bowery among the semi-deserted stalls. Down, past the Boardwalk, at muscle beach, the young and virile of both sexes now compete.

At amusement parks, male strength is closely allied to female fears, so the tunnel rides evolved into the Spook House and Hell Hole. Outside, painted faces of The Damned shriek at the customers or a maniacal laugh warns of horrors inside where spiders and skeletons fall in front of suspecting riders. Women cuddle close in the arms of their protectors and their eyes grow wide in the artificial darkness.

Or the wax museum and its Murderers' Row. "Ooh, Donny, is that real blood? Did they really chop off Marie Antoinette's head? There's John Dillinger's death mask. And Bonnie and Clyde. Did that one man kill all those women? What did he do to the bodies? Hold me tight. This is creepy." And the Siamese twins. Here's the girl who gave birth when she was five years old—and was a grandmother at 15?

The Eden Musee opened in 1916 with exhibits in "ceroplastic art": "Murder for a Thrill," the Leopold/Loeb murder of Bobby Franks; Horrors of the Spanish Inquisition; An Opium Joint; Death of Julius Caesar; the death masks of Martin Luther, Napoleon I, Dante and Ludwig van Beethoven; a nursing mother. The quality of the subject matter did not elevate much beyond this level and frequently fell much lower. Other wax museums came and went.

Perceiving a high interest in the abnormal during the nineteenth century, P.T. Barnum started a circus (with a sideshow), followed by Ripley's "Believe It or Not." Coney Island joined them.

Freaks!

"Hurry, hurry, hurry. Step right up and see the ugliest man in the world, so ugly that his mother disowned him at birth. Zip, the pin-head boy, and later the twin pin heads, Zipo and Pipo. And the purple man. Or the rubber lady who can scratch her head with her toes. Cannibals, headhunters. The snake lady. The dog-faced boy. The elephant man. The strangest couple in the world: he's 7-foot, 5; she's less than 3 feet. How do they ever get together? You gotta see it to believe it!"

Samuel Gumpertz specialized in gathering the largest assortment of abnormal humans in

Girl on Merry-go-round

Boarded Bowery in March

one exhibit: at Dreamland, the White City by the Sea. Hundreds of undersized people lived in his midget city named Lilliputia, a model of Germany's Nuremburg. But Gumpertz' exotic sideshows of Eskimaux (the popular spelling), Philippine headhunters and freaks drew even more awe-struck crowds. After Dreamland's fire, he continued with sideshows and expanded to other cities. Eventually, he moved over to Ringling Bros., Barnum & Bailey.

At both Dreamland and Luna Park, across the street, were Incubator Baby shows. Supervised by a legitimate medical staff, infants were cared for in sanitary exhibits which saved many lives of the premies. Since incubators were not readily available in hospitals, the demand for this free care was great and visitors (at 10 cents each) flocked to watch the care from behind glass windows. In more recent times, the exhibit was reduced to caring for premature animals.

Sideshows-By-the-Seashore continues the carnival tradition today with Dick Zigun's guest freaks appearing at Coney Island, USA where "Alive!" is the motto: the tattooed man, the snake charmer, the sword swallower, the fat lady, the strong man. Watching them all is a thoughtful man, just three feet tall.

"Come one, come all. A new show every hour. See the strangest mistakes Nature ever made. Meet Jolly Trix, The Fat Girl: so fat it takes seven men to hug her. Hurry, Hurry, Hurry!"

The catchpennies of yesterday exchanged their 3-card monte decks for Skeeball, Bingo, Keno and Fascination arcades. Coney Island once had three *major* race tracks: now the horses are confined to arcade races. The only real horses are ridden by the police.

In Coney Island, the operation of games of "chance" has been controlled by a select monopoly of families who run the arcades. The rules of the games are the same; only the players have changed. Operators of these flat games have carny blood in their veins: every player is a sucker. The "come on" is still in the pitch. In the '30s, hucksters hawked, "Take home a Charlie McCarthy," referring to the popular ventriloquist dummy offered as a prize. In the '60s, they barked a new spiel: "Come on in, roll 'em up. Ladies have the gentle touch. Eddie's Fascination, 10 cents. Any game, you win dollars worth of merchandise. Four packs cigarettes a quarter." Today they have added, "Mira, mira, mira."

If the weighted balls (to throw off the lucky winner) aren't enough, there's always the shill to con the rubes by winning the over-sized stuffed bear. "Gaffing," or fixing a game to allow a shill to win, is not unheard of. Wheels of Fortune, or plush wheels because the prize is a plush toy, have been known to stop on a dime.

Many of the games have origins in ancient fairs and traveling carnivals, and are more difficult than they appear: tossing games include block pitch, glass pitch, cane rack. Rules require rings to lie flat and coins to stay in the glass. Everybody wins in the string game, but the big prizes seldom move. The basket joint uses specially taut baskets that bounce softballs back at the thrower. In order to win the player must put a spin on the ball. Most popular has been the milk bottle, cat or dish pitch in which the odds of knocking over or breaking the target are more deceptive than they look. Other popular stands are the fish tank and balloon darts.

Then there's that grand prize—the elusive goal isolated at the top of the prize case. Regular customers return daily to win it. Usually it's a watch or camera, a piece of junk in any other setting. The prize is changed when it begins to show age.

Bowery Action in August

Winning the Prize

The jabber, and the dodges, continued into the forties. "Hurry! Hurry! Hurry! Only a quarter for three rolls of the ball or four packs of cigarettes. Take a chance. You can't lose!"

TV booths of the '50s supplemented the arcades, just as video games do today. New shops put pictures and words on "all I got was lousy" T-shirts.

But still the little boy with the big plush giraffe or the lovers with a giant panda between them represent success at Coney Island. And if you can't win them, there's always the storefront with balloons, beach toys and even bigger stuffed animal pets—for sale.

Roman candles, flying fish, pinwheels, monster rockets. "Ooooohs" and "Aaaaahs" echo over the sands as the firework barges discharge their wares into the cloud cover.

It's the Fourth of July at Coney Island and cordite makes noses twitch.

Six million visitors still are drawn to Coney Island, claims *Newsweek*. Not an inch of sand can be seen between blankets.

Well, maybe several inches these days.

But Coney still has the drawing power. Pinpoint paratroopers descend on the beach as Blue Angels zoom among jet streams above and a military band blows out martial airs. The boardwalk and sand are thronged with squinting spectators peering upward. The military heroes later walk among their admirers. At night, fireworks light up Coney Island's sky on Independence Day and then every Tuesday and Saturday at 9 p.m.

It's coming back.

Nothing changes.

Fireworks have long been the hallmark of the amusements. The first—staged by the Pains of London, Henry and James—entertained the Manhattan Beach crowds in 1879. No mere firecracker show, they incorporated live historical dramas, usually involving a sea battle, with hundreds of actors, acrobats and extras. This ended in the defeat of the Spanish Armada, the pirates of Tripoli, the Mexicans at Vera Cruz, the Russians at Sevastapol or the Spanish navy in the Philippines. The Marines were victorious.

Then barges and shore works set off a vast display including fiery tributes to the contemporary celebrities: presidents, queens, military heroes. Following this, the crowds drifted off to the band concerts given by Gilmore, Sousa, Pryor, Levy, Herbert before heading for the last boat home.

The Pain fireworks were made on Manhattan Beach with several warehouses situated in Brooklyn and Staten Island. Brighton Beach and West Brighton followed with their own firework show—also created by the Pain organization.

Today we have the Grucci family to create jingoistic pyrotechnics.

While the Coney Island fireworks signal the opening of the summer season, the Mardi Gras parade marks the end. Started at the beginning of the century by Louis Stauch (of Stauch's Baths), the original purpose was to raise money for the reconstruction of a home for "wayward girls" that had burned. The competition for floats pressured the competitive instincts of Coney Island businessmen. Revived by Richard Egan and Dick Zigun, it still attracts crowds as it snakes along Surf Avenue with its crowned King Neptune and Miss Mermaid.

Today, though, the elements of crime—pickpockets, rowdies, mashers—that accompanied the initial parades are missing. No matter how undesirable conditions are today, the crime in the Coney Island of the past accounts for the moniker used by *The New York Times*, "Sodom By the Sea."

Today, New Yorkers have learned to live with

Memorial Day Parachute Jump

The Labor Day Crowd

crime. But we feel reasonably well-protected. During summers, the streets and boardwalk of Coney Island are patrolled on foot, on horse, on motor skooters, in cars and in vans. Police in helmets mingle with the visitors in baseball caps, yarmulkes, straw sun hats. The beachgoers feel confident enough to sit on benches with strangers, to lounge there, to socialize. If an event promises unprecedented crowds, additional police are sent from other precincts.

In the days before the City of Brooklyn annexed the Town of Gravesend, law and order in the Coney Island section was selective. In some areas, there was neither.

Fugitive criminals wanted in other sections of Brooklyn, New York and New Jersey were safe from prosecution in Coney Island. Naive tourists who wandered from the key amusement area endangered their property and their lives. The Gut, behind the Brighton Beach Race Course, was notorious for its licentiousness: dance halls, prostitution, petty thievery, alcohol and drugs.

In the 1870s, visitors were accosted by 3-card monte dealers, street walkers, pickpockets. A favorite ruse was to guess the weight of a newcomer by touching various body parts, thereby determining the location of his billfold. Then an accomplice would go to work. Signs warning of pickpockets greeted the visitor from the moment he boarded the train or boat.

Initially, one or two Metropolitan police were assigned to Coney Island; then, the political boss, "Chief" John Y. McKane, campaigned to have the police appointed by him and dispatched by him. After the state granted his request, some of the same criminals hiding in Coney Island found themselves keeping order in blue uniforms as special patrols. Prostitution and gambling were not crimes in the Town of Gravesend. The Brighton race track, near police quarters, was the most corrupt.

Mounted Police

The Chevy

Punks

Girl with a Gun

Danger and Baby Carriages

Boardwalk Break-in

Asking Directions

Lost Dog

The Gossips

Sportland

62 AMUSEMENTS

Photo Studio

Polaroid Man

After the Ride

The Swings on Irish Day

The Carrousel

The Sweeper

68 AMUSEMENTS

After reformers reversed the criminal tide and sent McKane to prison for fixing elections, the quality of life in Coney improved under the Brooklyn and then New York municipal governments, even though Al Capone, Villa Joe and Frankie Yale worked the beach at times. They were legitimate businessmen. As the amusements became the center of Coney Island life, criminal behavior diminished.

Morty Dagowitz, who worked the arcades as a teenager during summers, claimed that often he was short at the end of a day supervising the Skeeball games, not because he shortchanged the customers, but because the customers ripped him off.

On the other hand, Tilyou never used security guards at Steeplechase; he believed that people out to have fun would not be dishonest. But he did fence in his park, just to be sure.

Half Moon Hotel

Childs' Building

THE BOARDWALK

he Boardwalk in Atlantic City claims to be the world's first: June 26, 1870.

But the term "boardwalk" is an Americanism for the British promenade. And the prime activity in Coney Island for much of its 150 years has been strolling. Early paths covered with sedge grass saved promenaders from getting sand in their shoes. A short, three-block boardwalk listed on mid-century maps was built for the same purpose. A nineteenth century boardwalk ran along The Bowery—a private entrance to Steeplechase—not near the ocean, for the hotels and amusements ran down to the shoreline preventing the structure of a seaside promenade. Then sand was added to the beach and amusements were moved back.

The first section of today's Reigelmann's Boardwalk, named after a Brooklyn borough president, was completed in 1923. Instantly, this strollers' paradise found acceptance, except for those who preferred the rolling chairs—for 50 cents an hour, an impractical fee after the minimum wage law was passed. Original plans called for the boardwalk to be extended to the tip of Manhattan Beach, but after the Brighton Beach section was finished in the mid-1930s, the promenade was pronounced complete. The future Steeplechase plans to construct a promenade over part of the existing boardwalk section.

Now, beach visitors can shop or swim or just hover over the sunbathers and kibitz from the boardwalk. Or instead of lying on the hot, crowded sand, they can stretch out on the boardwalk and sleep. Perhaps even play checkers. Mahjongg was a popular beach game—until Parks Commissioner Moses ordered the gambling to cease and the Brighton grandmothers to be fined.

Mounted police still patrol the boardwalk and even cop cars and ambulances occasionally climb the ramps to perform some mysterious civic duty.

Sometimes it's just to gaze at the bathing apparel and its inhabitants. Or to ticket an illegal bicyclist. Maybe chase a stray dog.

Children not being held by an adult's hand race along the geometric lines and someone always picks up a splinter. Baby carriages pushed by mothers have replaced the original rolling chairs pushed by teenagers. Lovers drape themselves over the rails, deep in personal discussion. Others dance to music from a radio. Teenagers with flat-topped, designed haircuts silently watch another group pass, those with shaved heads and hanging chains. Up the ramps and down the stairs go the straw hats carrying chairs, inner tubes, mats, coolers on the shoulders. A sanitation worker sweeps paper into a bin.

A lone girl runs down the boardwalk.

Several years ago, Jacques d'Amboise, the dancer, staged a children's dance program at the Felt Forum called "A Day at Coney Island"; he imitated Coney Island scenes and used a backdrop painted by Brooklynite David Levine.

Amateur artists and professional salesmen line their wares along the boardwalk against a wall-sized mural: scenes of Coney Island, of Manhattan sights, of patriotic significance, of saucer-eyed children and animals. Others set up easels to sketch caricatures or chalk likenesses.

Among the first artists who gravitated to Coney Island were the men who cut silhouettes with scissors and black paper. These were followed by the first daguerreotype photographs or tintypes, initially taken by wandering photographers who set up tents. "Nine times out of ten," claimed a contemporary article, "the gipsy photographer gives you the best picture you ever had." Then shops grew along the boardwalk for funny photographs posed behind cutouts. Arcade photo booths attracted groups of teenagers seeing if they could all squeeze into the frame of a four-

Jasmine

74 THE BOARDWALK

Strolling the Boardwalk

for-a-quarter.

Now, lifesize cutouts of national celebritics will pose with visiting nobodies. Or you can mount a stuffed tiger or other beast of the wild for a Polaroid snapshot.

Professional photographers still use Coney Island for subject material: Weegee framed his famous photo there of the packed beach people waving to him. Movie cinematographers stage scenes among the sights. Now Lynn Butler has found her inspiration there.

    Among the rides.

    On the streets.

    At the beach.

    Under the Boardwalk...

Once upon a time Coney Island had three grand hotels of over 400 rooms each: the Manhattan Beach, the Oriental, and the Brighton Beach. Literally hundreds of others dotted the strip.

Once there was an elephant who lived in a hotel. Or perhaps it was vice-versa. At least the hotel, if that's the right term, was called The Colossal Elephant. A roller coaster encircled it. People entered the rear legs to the rooms above. Talk was that it became a naughty place for shameless women who procured weak-willed men. Then it burned down, one night. The new Steeplechase wants to reintroduce an animated pachyderm.

Now there's the Underwood Hotel, for those lovers who can't afford a hotel room. And for today's shameless hussies and amoral men. Pat Benetar sang about Coney Island whitefish. The Drifters sang about the Boardwalk. And lovers still watch submarine races from Under the Boardwalk. Only today we have learned to call condoms by their right name.

A girl stands clasped by a boy's legs. Couples embrace on the hood of a parked car. The garish night lights reflect silhouettes. A blanket moves.

Some things never change.

Up above are other empty shells: used, abandoned or discarded, cast aside.

Stauch's Baths—once the home of Louis Stauch, who worked at Coney Island from his teenage years. He built it in the days when visitors came to Coney Island for the social camaraderie: swimming, dancing, indoor games, food, people watching. Dancers used to circle the dance floor to the turkey trot—the dirty dancing of its day—while bachelor girls draped themselves over the balcony tables watching. Just watching. Later, in the basement Turkish baths, gays gathered in the steam rooms. Just watching. Graffiti from the film "The Warriors" was splashed over its exterior. The roof has collapsed, letters from his name have fallen with the building.

Child's Restaurant—the shell of the boardwalk's first restaurant and building at West 21 Street still resembles the exotic frame that was constructed there in 1923. Name bands used to play there for rooftop dancing under the stars. Now, hourly workers fashion chocolates.

Half Moon Hotel—built by Samuel Gompers before The Great Depression as a working class showpiece of a newly rehabilitated Coney Island. Then financial chaos and the infamous penthouse prison of Murder, Inc. hit-man-turned-stool-pigeon Abe Reles—a.k.a. Kid Twist—until he flew—or fell—to his death below. During World War II, an r & r hotel for the military. Then, in peace, a geriatric home. Now, minus its globe top, a rehabilitation center.

The Parachute Jump and the Thunderbolt— hope for their rehabilitation rests in the plans for a new Steeplechase Park announced by Horace Bullard. The frame of the landmarked original Lifesaver Parachute Jump is to be strengthened; in recent summers, it has served as a challenge

Mother and Child on the Boardwalk

Running the Boardwalk

for urban mountain climbers who annually scaled its frame to fly a flag of victory from its peak. The new park is to have a flag flying from that point.

The Thunderbolt, last seen in "Annie Hall," has been purchased by Bullard. More rickety than The Cyclone, they said. Attached to the southern end of the roller coaster the home of Fred Moran and Mae Timpano had been constructed on the foundation of the old Kensington Hotel. The couple lived among the rumble and roar, unmarried because his mother didn't approve. Moran died and Timpano, ironically, nursed his mother there for the balance of her days.

Bullard claims the old roller coaster skeleton is unsalvageable, but he intends to incorporate an attraction called Mae's Story-Telling Theater, in which stories of old Coney Island, illustrated by pepperghosts, would be recounted while sounds of a roller coaster rumbling by echoes and rattles the screen.

These ghosts of the more recent years of Coney Island still haunt the shoreline. Most of the older amusements succumbed to fire before mid-century. But Coney's reputation for food outlasts them all.

FOOD AND DRINK

Another typical scene:

"C'mon, sport, buy me another glass of champagne."

The woman flounced her petticoats and ran a finger over the man's collar. He faced her, trying to focus on her painted features. As she leaned over the man, letting him breathe in her perfume, she tipped a vial of liquid into his glass. The mustached bartender grinned as he placed a drink in her hand.

"Here's to good ol' Coney Island," she toasted.

The man looked up, his eyes bleared. "Here's to..."

As he gulped a swallow, his glass fell to the floor and he sank to the brass foot rail. Two men emerged from the shadows to drag the unconscious one out the swinging doors.

The bartender motioned the woman to another single man further down the bar.

Thrills and women were said to be the primary reasons for visiting Coney Island for over a hundred years. The morphine-dispensing saloons of The Gut were attacked by Carry Nation and Anthony Comstock and cadres of reform preachers and politicians. Soon, the Raines Law required food to be sold with drinks.

But food had been a prime attraction before Coney Island became a symbol for mechanical rides. Champagne and shore dinners attracted the upper classes who dallied after the races at the Manhattan Beach and Oriental Hotels over six-course feasts, then swam at the electrically illuminated beach or listened to classical music played by a symphonic band. The Rhode Island clam-bakes and kegs of beer at the Sea Beach Palace, Tilyou's or Vanderveer's drew the immigrant and working class masses. The Brighton Beach Hotel supplied champagne on tap to the middle-class patrons for ten cents a glass.

Not all food was for sale. In the early days,

Moon over Fulton's

Nathan's

excursion parties staggered over the sands with wicker picnic baskets, much as husky, shirtless men today carry beer coolers. German families toted hampers full of bread, home-made sausages, pickles, fruit.

Hotels advertised their excursion pavilions, or picnic tables, which were set apart from those used by the regular hotel patrons. At those tables, the day trippers could spread out their feast and indulge. Of course they needed beer, which the waiter would gladly supply. Or if party cared for an additional platter of food—fish, for example?

For a price.

Again, if families didn't mind the sand and the hot sun and the peddlers, they could lay a cloth on the sand and indulge there, at no cost.

Some Germans swarmed around the West Brighton restaurants, namely Bauer's West Brighton Hotel and Feltman's Ocean Pavilion. To introduce a touch of the homeland to his countrymen, Charles Feltman entertained them with the Liederkranz singing societies, in the Deutscher Garten dining room and, as a specialty, with a sausage he placed between two slices of bread and called a frankfurter.

Cartoonists labeled it "hot dog."

Today Nathan's Finest has co-opted the reputation as the home of the red hots. Nathan Handwerker had worked in Feltman's kitchen and eventually opened his own stand down the street, under and outselling his former employer.

But Nathan's has everything, not only red hots, according to Coney Island gourmands: the best pastrami in the history of the world, unparalleled french fries, succulent hot sweet corn, crisp lobster rolls and tangy clams, juicy kosher pickles, bubbly root beer. And more shrimp boats than New Orleans. The cars triple parked, revving their engines on Surf Avenue in front of Nathan's, which proves that the gustatory skill has not been lost.

Boardwalk Ice Cream

Food tastes have expanded, so these days the demand for ethnic foods surpasses the taste for the native American clams and corn. The Italian restaurant, Gargiulo's, has served a southern Italian menu since the 1920s. Carolina's, around the corner, has reopened its Italian kitchen. Pizza is sold at boardwalk stands, just as Feltman served his frankfurters. Joining these grab joints with instant meals are the Yiddish knishes, Middle Eastern falafal and Turkish shish kebabs. Now Russian pastilias and other specialties can be tasted at Brighton Beach's Odessa-By-the-Sea.

More junk food than the Surgeon General recommends can be purchased at the multitude of stands that line the visitor's path from the Stillwell Avenue station to the end of the boardwalk: popcorn, both caramel sticky or salted; crispy-coated green apples; colored ice named slush; bananas covered with hardened imitation chocolate; pink, adhesive, air-filled cotton candy; banana-flavored frozen custard.

One custard stand owner relished watching black girls eat his banana custard, contrasting the yellow with the color of their skin. Introduced in the 1940s by buxom young women barkers crying, "We pile 'em sky high, creamy and deee-licious," custard, or soft ice cream, caught on quickly.

And Eskimo Pie? Everybody knows it was cooked up in Coney Island freezers.

But corned beef sandwiches have lost popularity along with the Irish tenor singing waiters at Joe's Famous Restaurant, the Irish House and Gilsey House who have been silenced, and the Sodamat no longer dispenses nickel sodas. Ruby's open bar, the only bar left on the boardwalk, is still accessible, though, its American flag over the bar and pictures of the past lining the walls.

Ruby's—a cavern on the boardwalk, off

Stillwell. A coterie of gruff-looking, baseball-capped men sit at tables outside, swapping tales of treasures found and lost in the sands of Coney. A stranger walks by, asks a question. "Boy, you shoulda seen the old days!" A couple in shorts enters the dark, cool interior, sit on barstools and order drafts from Ruby's brother, Phil. They gaze at the wall, nailed end-to-end with photos and enlarged post cards, as moist glasses of beer with Coney Island heads are placed in front of them.

"See that building to the right?" says Ruby Jacobs, a stocky man in his sixties, hair parted in the center. "That was the ballroom at Luna Park. And that Child's restaurant was a firewall that once stopped all Coney from burning to the ground."

The woman comes from Australia. She heard about Coney down there. Now she's here. The past meets the present.

From a dark corner, Barry Manilow suddenly drowns out all conversation. Ruby leaves to adjust the jukebox volume.

In front, the food stand attracts bathing-suited customers, towels wrapped around their midriffs. Fresh corn. Hot dogs. Now chimichangas, in deference to new tastes. Asian tourists approach, cameras ready.

The men sprawl around the table, cap bills pulled over their eyes, seldom smiling. The three-foot midget joins them. Used to work at Steeplechase. An ambulance rumbles by cautiously, lights twirling. Aroused, they talk about the probable cause, compare passersby to images from the past, and retreat into silence. Two gaze past the strollers and bathers, out to sea.

Nothing changes.

The Musicians

88   FOOD AND DRINK

Polar Express at Night

THE BEACH

Beach, anyone?

Surf, sand and sun seem so natural to us that we scarcely know that it was otherwise. Now we prepare in tanning salons, with pre-tan cream and sun block. Swim suits have their own issue of *Sports Illustrated*. Sun worshippers see themselves in these costumes, even if their flesh rolls over the edges. Armed with blankets, umbrellas, chairs, radios, beer and sunglasses they scrape along the boardwalk to find a patch of sand on which they can prostrate themselves to the sun. Theirs is not to thrill to the rides but to ogle and be ogled at. For it is obvious their sunning suits would not prevail in a pounding surf. But there are others.

Many still bob up and down, screaming, as the surf crashes over and around them. Or swim beyond the breakers until the lifeguard shrills his whistle.

Then they dance across the hot sands, back to their blankets and their radios where they glisten with sun oil and whiten their noses with more sun block. They lie on their stomachs; bras are unhooked and straps eased off the shoulders. They sleep. The beach waves as a forest of arms and legs.

Men and women expose as much of the human body to the sun as is socially acceptable. There is no pride, except in the perfect form. They press, and pull, and starve, and shave, and wax, and color, and redo themselves so they can represent a fictional ideal. As more of the body is exposed, more of it must be disciplined.

And no one is arrested.

Before the 1870s and rapid transit to the beach, people found summer entertainment other than the beach—such as saloons and fairs and parks. Men who wished to swim would bathe *au naturel*. Women would suffer.

Then behavior codes reversed themselves

and bathers even wore bathing sandals to swim. Women expressed shock at the sight of an exposed, ugly male toe!

Two types of bathing costumes were appropriate for women: one in which to frolic in the surf, covered from the neck to the ankles; the other, more form-fitting, with tights above the knees and shorter sleeves. As today, one was more practical than the other. Men, too, were required to wear tops on Coney Island's beach until 1935. Only within the confines of the private baths could men expose their chests. Many felt that, without rules, Coney would be transformed into the world's most notorious nudist beach.

Once the pleasures of Coney Island were discovered, another industry developed: bathing suit rental and bath house rental. The first bath houses were closet-sized rectangles, with knotholes for voyeurs. These grew into gargantuan, multi-storied emporiums with shops, games, entertainment and a laundry for the rented swimwear. Only when less cumbersome bathing suits were accepted did bathers design to wear their suits under their beach clothes and become the "wet seat set."

But the first ladies who dared to swim without stockings were assured a lecture from a patrolman, if not an arrest. The press, such as a *Brooklyn Eagle* editorial, appealed for less material in bathing suits. By the time women were enfranchised, the coverage receded until everyone wondered where it would stop.

It stopped in a bikini—a teensy, weensy polka dot bikini, as described by a Brooklynite song writer who obviously had visited Coney Island in summer.

As soon as the masses accepted the beach as their rightful property, as soon as the layers of clothing were thinned out, as soon as the public became aware of the shape of the human body,

Helicopter Ride

Looking into Hell Hole

people demonstrated their prowess for making fools of themselves. Early Edison films from Coney Island show lines of young men and women cavorting in silent frivolity: human pyramids, leap frog races, runs through the surf. Then came the beauty parades on the boardwalk and at Tilyou's, which claimed it introduced the beauty parade—for grandmothers.

While some people frolicked in the Atlantic waters off southern Brooklyn and strutted on the boardwalk, others considered a day at the beach a workday—the lifeguards. Early brochures advertised "rough-and-readies," or lifeguards at the many private bath houses that lined Coney's shore. They were more likely to be in surf boats than on high chairs. Coney has always had a serious undertow and lifeguards were prepared to cope with the many inexperienced swimmers. Doctors were interviewed in newspapers for health rules about bathing.

The baths became cabanas with indoor swimming pools; regulars returned annually. Cook's and Washington Baths were the last two. In the 1950s, the Washington still charged only ten cents. Now the entire beach has become the bath house, with nudity attempted at times. No longer does modesty prevent a public change from wet to dry clothes. Suits on Muscle Beach are stretch fig leaves; the more body exposed, the better.

Beneath heaving blankets, lovers don't bother to retire under the boardwalk or wait until dark. The ubiquitous radio blasts its rap rhythms across the sand. No more are beachgoers adjured what *not* to do; now they can do anything *except*... (The Moses' "NO" signs were removed by the 1970s.)

On the adjacent blanket, purple-haired grandmothers speak in accents while squatting with the cribbed baby under the umbrella's shade, while other children still tunnel down to China...or at least until they strike water. By the waterline, turreted castles are still constructed by juvenile engineers, to be disfigured and demolished by the incoming tide. As the fathers sleep or pretend to listen to a baseball game, the mothers chatter with an occasional warning to an errant child.

Slogging through the hot sands comes the peddler. "Ice cream, get yer ice cream here. Cold sody. Ice-cold beer." On his head sits a handkerchief, the four corners knotted. Another, spotted with sweat, is around his neck. His hairy legs protrude from cutoffs and end in high-top sneakers. At his waist is a change apron with *Daily News* printed on it. No shirt. "Ice cream. Ice-cold beer and soda. Get it while it's hot."

Most amusement areas are abandoned in winter. In Coney Island, where the long winter shadows transform Fred Trump's Luna Park Houses into gaunt tombstones, a coterie of faithful habitues still walk the boardwalk, burrowed in coats. The big rides close, shuttered with steel doors, it's true, but parts of Astroland and some stands—including the ever-present Nathan's—remain open all year. In a picture, a lone ice cream lover enjoys outside Nathan's winter doors.

The sea gulls prance and reclaim *their* beach.

In December, January and February, a small group of mostly elderly, paunchy men (women have now joined them) disturb them, though; they march down to the deserted beach, remove their warmups, and—arms overhead—run noisily into the frigid waters. The Polar Bear Club has a declining membership but they, too, are part of the Coney Island life. They have no plans to change their habits.

Life is just a circle.

Nothing changes.

Bathers with Hose

96 THE BEACH

Nude Bather

SURROUNDING COMMUNITIES

The outskirts of Coney Island also benefited from the amusement park. The disreputable West End transformed into the millionaires' colony of Sea Gate in 1894. At first, it was the domain of a yacht club with houses designed by Stanford White and a lighthouse erected by the Coast Guard, then an artists' colony. In a burst of World War II patriotism, Lindbergh Park was renamed after a real hero, Colin Kelly, the first pilot killed. Now Sea Gate is an outpost of Hasidic families buttressed against the hordes of public bathers outside the guarded gates.

Manhattan Beach, once the restricted province of anti-Semite Austin Corbin, now is fronted by Holocaust Park at the tip of Sheepshead Bay. Luxurious homes in which some minor celebrities live still line the arbored streets through which summer crowds file to the most over-used public beach in the city. The eastern tip where a merchant marine base stood for half a decade during World War II now is occupied by a multi-million dollar unit of City University of New York: Kingsborough Community College. Over 10,000 students flock to classes there, where thousands of dancers once trucked and lindy hopped to 1930s big bands.

North, across placid Sheepshead Bay—named after a once-plentiful fish—a semi-dormant village rests, waiting for a real estate boom that may never arrive. Once the watering place of swells and sports who frequented the Sheepshead Bay Race Track and gourmet restaurants there, the town has hibernated while prosaic housing replaced the Victorian mansions that formerly stood there.

East of Sheepshead Bay, among the inlets and streams that flowed through that section of Brooklyn, hamlets and summer cottages have been converted into year-round bastions for white middle-class Brooklynites. Plumb Island, near

Dead Horse Inlet, once prospered with a hotel, general store, beach and ferry. Now, all that remains are the beach plum bushes and federal park sand next to the buzzing Belt Parkway. Mill Island became the Mill Basin community, famed for expensive homes with rarely-used docking space in place of back yards.

These bedroom communities now seem a world apart from the pizzazz of Coney Island that once was intertwined with their lifestyle. They have turned their backs on the fading glitter, on the minorities isolated there, on the geriatric citizens, on the failing businesses, empty lots and boarded up houses—only reacting when reference is made of transforming Coney Island into an Atlantic City-type gambling center.

So, once again, Coney Island stands alone, as it did in its heyday when it was shunned as a pariah.

The Polar Bear Club

CONEY ISLAND EXPERIENCE

The Coney Island Experience. What is it? Coney Island materialized as a resort, when average recreation was found in the corner saloon. Then, only the rich could afford to "get away" for more than a day—usually Sunday. Transportation made accessibility to Coney Island a reality for the masses. As the fares lowered, immigrant working people took advantage of the escape from the drudgery of morose city life. Descending from the trains and trolley cars, they entered a fantasy world—even if just for a few hours. They found a liberal, exciting spirit that was not part of their European life style. When they joined the Coney Island world, the rich left, creating a more unified, less stratified society there.

The very thought of bathing in *public* with the opposite sex!

This concept carried over into the amusements that were being created in the fertile minds of inventors: Thompson, Tilyou, Edison, Mangels. The Industrial Revolution had opened a new, exciting world for the average man.

Americans suddenly were able to travel faster than ever, be carried higher in space, to take greater chances, to see exotic new worlds and peoples. This instinctive reaction made visitors proud to be Americans, created a jingoistic attitude. A national fervor developed for Coney Island as a home of a world's fair, a permanent carnival. On summer weekends, cares of reality would be swept away.

Bit by bit, this reaction eroded. As long as a depression encircled us—such as those in the 1890s, the 1920s and 1930s—Coney Island worked. But slowly, automobiles whisked tourists to Long Island and New England and Florida. Then planes. Then electricity brought us, not only lights for Coney's Electric City, but radio and movies and television—and air conditioning.

In wartime—World Wars I and II—Coney

Digging to China

Coney Island Skyline

again supplied an escape valve, a reminder for soldiers and sailors home on leave, "On the Town." But by the end of the last "good" war, we no longer needed tawdry Coney Island. Money was easy, automobiles were plentiful, travel was fast and painless.

Great Adventure, Disney World, Hershey Park, Busch's Gardens, Seven Flags beckoned. "Come on down," they said. City politicians saw only an expanse of wasted land, so they decided to waste it more, virtually returning it to the "sand waste" of a hundred years before. Elaborate plans to develop a real estate project tripped and collapsed when the finances withered away. At the turn of the century, reformers had wanted to convert the island into a gigantic park; then the money ran out, diverted to building bridges from Manhattan to Brooklyn and Queens.

Today husks of buildings without services fill the old West End.

Still a core of amusements mark the center of Coney Island. It attracts those who have continued to go there out of habit. New immigrants still gravitate to the beach for the same reasons older ones did: it's cheap. Tourists still want to see Coney Island.

But former Brooklynites return, shake their heads, and say, "It ain't like it uster be."

Matt Kennedy, the president of the Coney Island Chamber of Commerce and son of a former Coney Island police hero, disagrees. He gestures at the new, single-family homes growing in a colony near the school. Coney Island, he says, has a permanence, a charm that will always attract the young-at-heart. It represents a universality, a desire to escape to an exciting world of fantasy.

Computers can grab you and hold on, but the excitement of a day swimming at the beach and an evening riding amusements is a real, not a vicarious thrill. The faces of those who ride home today with wet bathing suits haven't changed. They show the same excitement and pleasure in the present that the "old timers" recall.

Things change, but they don't change. Y'know what I mean?

The Future.

No one—not even Horace Bullard—is going to bring back the past. Coney Island will never again be the watering place of millionaires. We can never again place ourselves in the position of never knowing about electricity or television or jet travel. We can never relive our youthful experiences. We can never regain our virginity.

But.

The past is powerful. Bullard, or some philanthropist, could build a working, modern amusement park. Maybe, like the Aquarium and South Street Seaport, it could be a year-round site. Perhaps even one that has a section for authentic or rebuilt amusements—an historical park for classic rides. It could work, providing the excitement and escape for the millions who still travel to Coney Island's beaches.

Perhaps quality restaurants could be encouraged to relocate. And express train and bus service could be planned. How about a Surf Avenue trolley car? A real one. The balance of the Coney Island strip should be considered for what it is: prime, waterfront real estate, rather than desolation row.

The future might of course reach way into the past. On the other hand, maybe Coney Island will return to its true roots—a windswept, barren tidal island of cedar groves, sedge grass and rabbit (or coney) warrens.

Things can change. And sometimes, y' know, the more things change, the more they remain the same.

AFTERWARD: THE FUTURE

While the name Coney Island has long been a synonym for evil since the days of "Thunderbolt" Norton and "Chief" McKane, signs of cautious renewal are emerging. The most ambitious is the plan of Horace Bullard, who hopes and plans to rebuild a totally new Steeplechase Park on the site of George Tilyou's emporium. More reminiscent of Great Adventure than the original, it will, nevertheless, draw on historical names—Paul Boyton, L. A. Thompson, William Mangels, Goerge Tilyou—as well as on the more contemporary scenic railway, merry-go-rounds, circular rides and themes.

Bullard, a developer and entrepreneur, sees it as a family theme park superimposing historical concepts over the most recent amusement creations. Built on several levels, the two-block park will include a four-horse Steeplechase ride, an animated elephant, a reconstructed Parachute Jump, a Crystal Palace, the Luna Shuttle, Paul Boyton's Old Shoot-the-Chutes, Dreamland Puppet Theater, George Tilyou's Dynamic Theater and Broadway entertainment. With a 99-year lease and 47 rides and attractions on 10 acres of beach front and boardwalk property, how can it fail? Bullard feels that Coney Island is "breathing with art," so he intends to promote artistic endeavors. He expects visitors to take seven hours to exhaust his park.

All for *one* general admission price.

Landmarked attractions at Coney Island indicate that *someone* is paying attention: the Wonder Wheel, the Cyclone, Riegelmann's Boardwalk and the Parachute Jump have been preserved by law. Astroland and the New York Aquarium still attract summer throngs. Coney Island U.S.A., ever searching for creative new side shows, lures audiences into its nostalgia-filled museum and theater for drama by the seaside. The bell rings and children still gleefully ride

Rendering of Horace Bullard's Future Coney Island

the newly-painted steeds of the B&B Carousell. Restaurants—Gargiulo's, Nathan's, the renewed Carolina's—still make food-lovers salivate. Ruby's persists.

There are other signs of revitalization. The Astella Development Corporation, a quasi-official organization, is overseeing introduction of middle-class single-family housing and service industries, where only workers once lived. The group, financed by bonds, continues to fight the city's long tradition of dumping on Coney Island. With potential new political candidates, they pressure the city and business interests for attention, on the assumption that a seaside location should not be an urban garbage pit.

With steady effort, the entertainment, business and residential interests may be able to turn the tide. Offering a modicum of pleasure coupled with a viable community of residents should not be beyond reason, even in a return to the future.

And signs of that future are more than apparent.

Rear cover: *Coney Island Kaleidoscope*